COMMISSIONED!
Signed, Sealed & Delivered

Notary Public Loan Signing Agent
Field Guide

Deborah M Raiter

ISBN: 9781099523601

SPECIAL WORDS

A very special and eternal thank you to Jesus for His richest grace, blessings and guidance for the publication of this manuscript.

My deepest gratitude and heartfelt thanks to Shellie Dill, Dorothy, Gerald Jr., Gerald III, and Erinn Walsh, along with Sherry Ezell for their prayers, love, encouragement and support. I so love you all and thank you so, so much for always believing in me. :)

I would also like to acknowledge Rachel Arterberry for being the most amazing editor, proofreader and so much more. Additionally, I really want to acknowledge Valory Waligoski for her design help and ideas for the cover design. I feel both of these wonderful people came to the project God-Breathed and I am so grateful for you.

Acknowledging our journey together, a special thank you to you, the reader, for sharing this material with your friends, family and special connections.

KJV NUMBERS 6:24-26

IN JESUS'S NAME I PRAY

יְבָרֶכְךָ יהוה, וְיִשְׁמְרֶךָ
יָאֵר יהוה פָּנָיו אֵלֶיךָ, וִיחֻנֶּךָ
יִשָּׂא יהוה פָּנָיו אֵלֶיךָ, וְיָשֵׂם לְךָ שָׁלוֹם

**"THE LORD BLESS YOU
AND KEEP YOU;
THE LORD MAKE HIS FACE SHINE ON YOU
AND BE GRACIOUS TO YOU;
THE LORD TURN HIS FACE TOWARD YOU
AND GIVE YOU PEACE."**

Table of Contents

Friendly Legal Notice and Financial Disclaimer

I am not a legal expert. The information that I have provided here, including outbound website links and any other accompanying material and resources are for education and informational purposes only. It should not be considered legal or financial advice. Also, while I do my very best to provide 'industry' financial outcome averages, I do not make any guarantee or other promise as to any results that may be obtained from using this content.

This information is furnished As-Is and is to be used at your own risk. It does not constitute legal advice or opinions of any kind, or any advertising or solicitation. Always check with your attorney or your state for current legislation, laws and regulations.

Thank you so much.

About the Author

Deborah M. Raiter is a Minnesota-native and a U.S. Navy Veteran, who has 20+ years of experience in real estate sales, management and ownership. She has supervised and witnessed 1000+ purchase, escrow and loan signings in her career.

As a former Air Traffic Control Specialist at one of the nation's busiest airports, she was trained on some of the most advanced technical systems, requiring exact attention to detail, communication and follow-thru.

As a result, Deborah has developed a unique passion for absorbing highly complicated, puzzling and mind-boggling situations, and breaking them down to simple, straightforward and easy to follow steps.

Deborah brings forward the breadth of her life experience in this simple and easy to understand quick start guide where you will learn to start, market and flourish as a part or full time Notary Public.

Getting Personal!

I share the information below with you to personalize this book, to offer hope in case you are in a dark place, and to be completely transparent.

I have been a very high-functioning individual for most of my life, maintaining careers that some might consider to be some of the most demanding, responsible and highest stress jobs in our developed country.

However, for over 50 years, I had suffered with depression, anxiety and panic. I became an alcoholic at an early age, developed disordered eating and was hospitalized twice. With a heart of service, I was constantly searching for God or something that had real meaning outside the mundane. This thrusted me full steam into the new age movement. I would have brief periods of peace and hope, only to be completely disillusioned. It was a labyrinth leading to a dead-end. I felt hopeless and functioned in a sort of purgatory of not wanting to live, and not wanting to die.

Then a Miracle!

In one of my darkest moments, I had the insight to reach out and have a friend pray for me. As she prayed, I was literally engulfed by an indescribable cloud of holiness, a radiant glory that awakened within me an unconditional love and connection with the Messiah, Jesus Christ. This was such a remembered, instinctive and eternal knowing. I cannot adequately describe in words what that kind of 'Love' is. His spirit realized within me, an instantaneous connection with the God I had been searching for my entire life. I knew within those moments that my search was over and that I would never be alone or experience darkness, depression or anxiety again.

Now, years later, I have a life that is purpose-driven in Christ, grace-filled and so unbelievably amazing, it is hard to find words to describe it. The depression, fear, anxiety, panic...all have been miraculously removed.

This has been so life-altering, I felt a need to share this story within this book, offering all those that read these words, hope in Jesus Christ....Deborah Raiter

To read my full testimony, please visit my website: www.sedonanotary.com/mystory.

A Notary Public Commission!

A notary public is a **commissioned** public official who performs valuable services to the legal, business, financial and real estate communities by certifying or witnessing signatures on official documents.

A **mobile** notary public is a notary public who travels to clients' homes, offices or mutually agreed upon public locations.

Why I Love It

I love this business because it is a recognized profession, I am a trusted public servant and I make a great living at it. Plus, I call my own hours, I am my own boss and I get to spend more time at home with my dog.

Benefits of Becoming
A Notary Public

- It is a profession
- Work-from-home
- Part or full Time
- Requires minimal start-up costs, usually less than $250 (assuming you have a computer)
- Flexible hours
- Independent contractor (which includes the tax benefits and write offs)
- No experience or college education required
- Unlimited amount of income potential
- Driving! Depending on how far you are willing to drive, you will have time in the car to listen to audio inspirational, training and other books and programs.

The Skills Necessary to Be a Great Notary

- Attitude of Gratitude
- Professional and Gracious
- Communicative
- On time/Prompt
- Attention-to-detail
- Service oriented
- Organized

The Cost

You can get started for as little as $250 (again, assuming you have a computer), which includes your state application, bond, insurance and office equipment.

Potential Income

You can make potentially an excellent living as a Notary Public, full or part time. State laws generally mandate the fees you can charge per *signature*; however, they normally allow a mileage and per diem charge.

As of March 2019, statistics show an average rate of $25 per hour as a general notary public. As a Loan Signing Agent (to be discussed later), you can earn anywhere between $75 to $300 per signing package, upwards of six figures a year. Your results may vary depending on your dedication, training and time available.

The Whys'!

Why I Am Sharing

The Business

This business, believe it or not, has been probably the most exciting work I have ever done. I say this with a history of over 20 years of real estate sales, management and ownership experience under my belt (you do not need any experience, by the way). It is easy to start and requires a minimal investment. With just a little bit of commitment, dedication and putting yourself out there, I truly believe you will be able find freedom and joy within this work.

The Personal

I decided to share my personal story with you, the reader to add a caring 'human element' to this book. Also, and most importantly, to give you **hope** if you are in a dark place, feeling defeated and/or completely overwhelmed.

What is Your Personal Why?

Knowing your personal 'why' will help you find meaning, clarity and literally stacks-your-deck to gaining personal fulfillment and freedom. Be mindful of *your 'why'* as you read, understand and absorb the material. Some of the questions you might ask yourself to unearth your 'why' might be:

- What's the purpose for doing this?
- What does success look and FEEL like?
- What do I ultimately want to achieve?
- What are my values?
- What drives me?
- Why am I interested in becoming a Notary Public?

What this Book is Not

It is **not** a get-rich-quick scheme. Like anything in life, you have to commit and *actually* work it.

Remember! This is not just about the business, it is about you (us), being honest, morally upright, helping each other and helping others. For me, being a Notary Public means, helping others, really listening, honesty, transparency, walking through fear (doing it scared), committing, having discipline, showing up and giving back.

The Basics

The History

Ancient Egyptian "scribes" were the earliest known chroniclers of official communication in recorded history. The tools of their craft were pigments, water pots and writing implements.

Scribes, one of the highest levels in the bureaucratic ladder, had the privilege of attending almost every noteworthy event in the empire, with the intent of keeping records. Any type of document which was to be archived including personal letters, diplomatic communications, wills, official proclamations, tax records, administrative, economic, and religious documents went through their hands.

The closing phrase of their ancient letters, "May you be well when you hear this," implies that the scribes not only wrote, but also read communications between two people. The recording of events was so highly valued that Pharaoh Tutankhamen even included writing equipment among the necessities he had with him for the afterlife.

What is a Notary Public in Today's World?

In today's world, a Notary Public is responsible for verifying the identity of a signer of important documents, confirming the signer's willingness to engage in the agreement and his/her awareness of content for which he/she is signing. Sometimes the notary may need to put the signer under oath. A Notary is commonly needed for property deeds, loan signings, wills, powers of attorney, etc.

A Notary Public is duty bound to **not** act in a situation where they have personal interest. They must be impartial. Notary Publics are official representatives of the state.

Responsibility and Professionalism

As a notary public you are considered a public officer and appointed by the state government. This is a position of public trust and should be embraced with integrity and the highest level of professionalism. Your primary role is to help prevent fraud and with it carries an enormous responsibility. You will more than likely be witness to transactions upwards of a million dollars.

Legal Risks to Consider

Notary Public notarial certifications are critically important and often involve hundreds of thousands, if not millions of dollars. This is why it is so important for you to follow state laws, get educated and professionally trained. Some of the legal risks involved include, but are not limited to:

- Notarizing a fraudulent or expired I.D.
- Not maintaining a notary journal
- Notarizing documents with blank spaces
- Notarizing signers who are not physically present
- Giving advice
- Operating under an expired commission
- Not thoroughly completing notarial certificates

This is why it is important to purchase Errors and Omissions Insurance (E & O). While every notarization is important, your exposure may vary. This insurance will protect you after the notarization occurs. Explained in detail later in this book.

The Details!

What is a Notarization or a Notarial Act?

Notarization is the official **process** by which documents are certified to be worthy of public trust and to provide further assurance of its authenticity, the legitimacy of a signer's signature, and that he/she acted willingly, is of sound mind and is actually *intending* the terms of the document to be in full force and effect.

Why is Notarization Important?

As mentioned above, the process of Notarization represents the legitimacy and trustworthiness of official documents. Although transactions occur countless times per day that do not require documents to be authenticated, some require additional verification of authenticity and trustworthiness. Notarization instills a level of undeniable and unspoken intention and commitment by the parties involved, providing an additional layer of attestation and substantiation.

How It Works (Examples)

General Notary Work

John Smith is selling his vehicle in Arizona and needs to have his automobile title notarized prior to selling. The Notary Public meets Mr. Smith at an agreed upon location, verifies Mr. Smith's identity, and confirms the automobile title is in his name. The Notary watches Mr. Smith sign the document, then places his/her seal on the title where prescribed.

Loan Signing Agent (To be discussed later)

Mr. and Mrs. Smith are purchasing a home. They must sign the closing paperwork that makes them responsible for the mortgage, title insurance and other responsibilities. The Notary Public comes to the closing appointment, verifies the signers' identity (Mr. and Mrs. Smith), watches them sign the documents, and then affixes his/her seal to the documents, where required.

Notarial Acts
You Might Perform

These are just a *few* notarial acts/certifications conducted by a Notary Public. Please do not consider this to be all-inclusive list. These are the basic acts.

- **Acknowledgment:** An Acknowledgment is the process that occurs when a document is presented to a Notary Public, the identity of the signer is proven and validated, and the contents and consequences are understood by the signer. The signer also acknowledges that he/she was in no means coerced or pressured to sign the document.
- **Jurat:** Also known as a "verification upon oath or affirmation" is a statement or an affidavit, attesting to the fact that the signer has sworn under penalty of perjury that the information in the document is accurate and truthful.
- **Certified Copy:** A certified copy/attestation is completely different from all other notarial acts. In fact, not all states authorize notaries to perform this act. In this process, you do not administer an oath or take an acknowledgement from the signer. Instead, you either witness or make a copy of the document and/or you compare the photocopy to the original, then certify or attest that the photocopy is a verified copy of the original. Also, of note, in some states, they do not authorize you to compare the photocopy with the original. In this case, if your state authorizes such, you are the person that actually makes the copy and attaches appropriate notarial certification.

Now that we know what a notary public and a notarial act are, below I will show you a brief introduction into the basic process.

What Does This Look Like in Real Life?

Generally, you'll be doing three things on each appointment.

- **You'll Screen** - You'll make sure the signer has a valid I.D., that they are the person represented, and then you'll confirm their volition and awareness.
- **You'll Journal** - You'll enter details about the signer and the type of notarial act performed in the journal and then you'll have the signer sign the journal.
- **You'll Certify** - Now you'll certify by placing your seal and signature on the document(s).

As a Notary Public, What Kind of Documents Would I be Notarizing?

This a basic list of some of the documents you may encounter along the way:

- Power of Attorney
- Birth, marriage and death certificates
- Divorce decrees
- Deeds
- Copy certifications
- I9s'
- Last Will and Testament
- Healthcare directives
- Jurats, oaths and affirmations
- Odometer readings
- Quick claim deeds
- Safe deposit inventory

Now that we've covered the basic details of what a Notary Public is and what they do, let's jump right into getting started.

Let's Get Started!

Here are two wonderful channels to help get your notary career off the ground. You will make an application directly with your Secretary of State.

- **National Notary Association (NNA)** Call them directly at 800-876-6827 or follow this link: https://www.nationalnotary.org/, click on **"Become a Notary."**
  - Through NNA, there is a link to you Secretary of State where you make a direct application.
  - Through NNA, you can purchase your bond (if required by your state), E and O Insurance, and supplies.
  - Once you have received your commission certificate from your state, email that to the NNA and they will ship out your notary seal.
  - The NNA also provides many other benefits (explained later) including loan signing certifications, in-depth education, access to the notary hotline and other perks.
- **Secretary of State -** The Secretary of State is responsible for overseeing notary commissions as well as authenticating the signatures of public officials and notaries public.

How Long will it take to get my Notary Commission?

To get your commission can take anywhere from a few days (expedited) up to 4 weeks.

Insurance You'll Need

- **Errors and Omissions (E and O):** E and O Insurance protects you financially if you are sued for making an unintentional error, or if a claim is filed against you.
    - In some states, it may not be required. It is recommended, however, to purchase a policy at a *minimum* coverage of $25,000.
    - The industry average is about $100,000. This can be purchased through the NNA, among other sources and the cost varies between $25 and $125, approximately.
- **Surety Bond:** A surety bond is a financial guarantee to a person or entity who loses money because of a Notary's misconduct or fraud, to be reimbursed up to the bond's limit. Of note, a surety bond does not protect the Notary and not all states require it.
    - Price - I purchased a $5000 bond through the NNA in Arizona for around $25.

Developing Your Brand

Developing your personal brand, along with ordering your business cards, developing social profiles and website design takes a little time and consideration. You can start these processes just as soon as you receive your commission and can be worked on concurrently to your ongoing training and certification.

Your Attitude

Seek to understand, rather than be understood and go ALL-IN! This is a business about harmonious relationships! Always try to be sincere, have the attitude of gratitude, say thank you, offer to help, **admit when you made a mistake and make it right. Have the courage to be vulnerable.**

Your Brand Channels

- Business Cards
- Website
- Social Media - (Facebook/LinkedIn)

Business Cards

Business cards are inexpensive and can be purchased online from companies such as Vistaprint.com. They offer thousands of templates that are easily editable; the customer service is reachable and very friendly. For more resources, visit my webpage at www.sedonanotary.com/notaryresources.

I continue to update this page regularly with resources and information.

Websites

You need a professional presence in cyberspace for many reasons, including:

- Establishes you as an authority
- Brand recognition
- Potential customers can find you!

Two Approaches to launching a website:

DIY (Do-it-Yourself). Examples,

- Godaddy.com
- Wix.com
- Square.com

Outsource a pro to do it for you. Examples,

- Upwork.com
- Fiverr.com
- Deborah Raiter (Me)
    - **Website Design:** I have trusted resources that can provide you with a beautifully designed website, that is keyword/SEO optimized for the notary business.
    - **Website Hosting:** I offer discounted state-of-the-art website hosting, which includes technical support, SEO, security and plugin services to friends, family and customers that have purchased this book.
    - Bill Soroka of Sign and Thrive Notary Training Course has resources as well. http://www.notarycoach.com

TIP: Remember to have your website Search Engine Optimized (SEO)

Social Media Presence

There are many benefits to having a business page within the social media matrix. Some perks include brand awareness, customer engagement, customer support and you have an instant outreach and access to millions of potential customers. I highly recommend the following social channels:

- Facebook - Business page
- LinkedIn - Profile

Training and Education

General Notary Vs Loan Signing Agent

I love both the general and loan signing aspects of the business. What I really appreciate about the general notary side is I am constantly meeting new and wonderful people, it is fairly straightforward, not very stressful and payment is usually immediate. For loan signing, I love the complexity, the rush, all the communication involved and the payout tends to be much greater.

What is a Loan Signing Agent?

A Notary signing agent is a commissioned notary that is hired as an independent contractor to make sure that loan, escrow and title documents are executed by the borrower or signer, notarized, and returned for processing.

As a loan signing agent, in my opinion, you should have a dedicated office space or corner in your home where you have enough room to setup your printer, office supplies and have an area where you can lay out, review and flag for signatures the signing packages, which can have an excess of 150 pages.

Basic Notary Public Training Resources

- National Notary Association (NNA) - The NNA has great content and up-to-date education, webinars, certifications and training
- Secretary of State

Advanced Training and Certifications

Now you can decide if you would like to take your training a little further. There are two certifications you can get that will help you earn high dollars. Note, you cannot become a Reverse Mortgage

Signing Professional (CMSP) until you are certified as a Loan Signing Agent (NSA).

Loan Signing Agent (NSA)

A Notary Signing Agent or NSA is a Notary who has special training to handle loan document signings. Title companies and signing services hire NSAs to deliver loan documents to borrowers, oversee the signing and return the documents.

Reverse Mortgage Signing Professional (CRMSP)

A Certified Reverse Mortgage Signing Professional (CRMSP) is a Notary Public and Loan Signing Agent that takes additional training about the reverse mortgage industry, mindset, and process to better service signers, closing agents, and loan officers. To become a CRMSP you are required to pass an intensive exam with a score of 90% or greater.

The ROI or return on investment is potentially much greater having these certifications, however it can be more complicated and stressful. You might like that, though. :)

Trusted resources who provide these types of certifications and training are listed further in this book.

What is the Cost of Becoming a Loan Signing Agent and/or Reverse Mortgage Signing Professional?

The typical costs associated with becoming a Signing Agent are between **$140** and **$200** depending on the vendor and excluding the commissioning costs and necessary supplies.

Note: If you decide to pursue a career as a notary loan signing agent, you'll need to bump up your office artillery. Here are a few more tools you will need:

General

- Obviously, a smartphone (Android/iPhone)
- Computer and/or laptop
- Dual-tray laser printer and toner (you will be able to print both letter and legal documents)
- Scanner
- Internet connection

Office Supplies

- Legal/letter sized paper
- Blue and black pens
- Paper clips
- Large document clips

Do I have to have Real Estate or Escrow Experience to be a Loan Signing Agent?

I have found that most escrow/title and signing companies require only a Notary Public Commission and E and O Insurance. However, it is critically important, in my opinion to get as much education and training as you possibly can from reputable sources. With that said, you can always leverage your life experience and do so in an open and honest way.

How to Become a Loan Signing Agent

After you have your commission certificate, check out these resources for training and certification:

- **National Notary Association (NNA)**
  https://www.nationalnotary.org/, click on "Become a Certified NSA". They provide several training and certification packages for new notaries.
- **Bill Soroka**, founder of www.notarycoach.com. His Sign and Thrive Notary Training Course explodes with information and up-to-date course material including:
  - **NSA** - Notary Signing Agent
  - **CRMSP** - Reverse Mortgage Signing Professional (training and certification)
- **Carol Ray's Notary2pro:** https://www.notary2pro.com/. She offers similar training and certifications. She and Bill Soroka often team up and provide online, real-time notary webinars and office meetings.

Marketing

This section covers various ways for you to get your name or company in front customers, signing, escrow and title companies.

Start by applying to different loan signing services (explained below), contacting escrow/title companies and mortgage brokers.

Signing Companies or Services

A signing service is a company that acts as a liaison between a client and a Notary Public with the intent to facilitate the signing and notarization of loan documents.

- o Join Facebook groups that are focused on signing company reviews
- o Notary Reviews...the Good, Bad and the Ugly
- o Join www.notaryrotary.com. They have an extensive list of signing companies and their respective reviews
- o Google loan signing companies and start completing applications and profiles

The benefits of using a signing company or service is they do all the front-end marketing and just connect you with vendor. However, with that said, they do take a pretty big slice of the money pie.

TIP: You should **not** have to pay to sign-up for any of these companies. If you are asked to buy-in, do your research as many very reputable signing companies are absolutely free.

TIP: www.notarycoach.com and www.notary2pro.com usually have lists of notary-approved signing companies.

TIP: Websites such as www.123notary.com offer rated signing company lists, as well.

Escrow Direct

Escrow Direct or Direct Escrow is when you market yourself and develop relationships with the escrow company/officer directly. You essentially eliminate the middleman (signing company/service).

I love working escrow-direct because it enables me to foster incredible relationships with the various escrow officers. The payout is usually very lucrative because you do not have the signing company middleman.

- o Drop your business card, resume and connect human-to human.

Your Website

- For general and loan signing notary work, as stated earlier, your online presence is key. Update your website to reflect your new credentials.
- Your future customers generally will Google 'mobile notary near me' or 'loan signing agent near me'. You'll definitely want to have your website keyword enabled and SEO friendly. I suggest registering your business with Google Business.

Social Media

- Update your Facebook business page and/or LinkedIn profile that describes your new credentials.
- Start sharing your social pages and on LinkedIn, start connecting with escrow officers and mortgage brokers

Networking Groups

- Consider joining a local business networking group such as BNI or the like

Chamber of Commerce

- The Chamber of Commerce is a wonderful way to connect and meet new people.

Business Cards

There is business to be had from the following companies and/or organizations. Stop in, introduce yourself and drop off business cards.

- ○ Escrow / Title Companies
- ○ Banks, Mortgage Brokers
- ○ Convalescent/nursing homes
- ○ Hotels
- ○ Jails/Prisons
- ○ Property management
- ○ Senior citizen centers
- ○ Funeral homes
- ○ Car dealerships
- ○ Law offices
- ○ Airports
- ○ Bail bond companies
- ○ Mortgage/Loan companies
- ○ Travel agencies
- ○ Churches
- ○ Banks
- ○ Hospitals
- ○ Estate Planning offices
- ○ Human resource dept.
- ○ Real Estate agencies
- ○ Post offices/centers

Additional Ways to Make Money as a Notary Public

Field Inspections

Field inspectors verify information about businesses. For example, a field inspector may be requested to verify that a particular business is in fact a credible business entity. This may be done by conducting a site visit, examining incorporation documents, speaking to employees and taking photos of the location.

What qualifications are needed?

Although no previous experience or qualifications are required in order to conduct field inspections, a background check may be conducted. Brief training is typically offered by most companies hiring field inspectors. In order to complete the inspection process, field inspectors will be required to have a reliable vehicle, a high-speed internet connection and a digital camera with a flash and time and date stamp capability.

How much does it pay?

Field inspectors typically earn between $18 and $40 for a typical inspection such as a business verification which usually requires 10-15 minutes.

How can I get started?

For additional information on becoming a field inspector, please contact The Society of Field Inspectors. If you are interested in becoming a photo inspector, <u>OnSource</u>, a company that provides photo inspection services to insurance companies, is interested in hiring notaries. An application is available on their website.

Process Servers

What is it?

A Process server is one who delivers or "serves" legal documents to individuals including subpoenas and other court-related documents.

What qualifications are needed?

If you are interested in becoming a process server, carefully examine the laws in your particular state since the regulating process varies from state to state. It is not uncommon for a jurisdiction to assess a fee to cover the cost of a background check, surety bond, or testing and licensing costs in order to become a process server.

How much does it pay?

Fees vary so be sure to confirm with your state or jurisdiction.

How do I get started?

For more information, contact the <u>National Association of Professional Process Servers</u> or your local state associations.

Form I-9 Services

What is it?

Due to the increasing number of remote employees being hired, companies are utilizing the services of an authorized representative to complete the Form I-9, Employment Eligibility Verification for its newly hired employees. The U.S. Citizenship and Immigration Services (USCIS) permits Notaries to conduct this verification process.

How much does it pay?

Because this is not a notarial act, there are no guidelines for fees to be charged and therefore, you are free to negotiate your rate.

What qualifications are needed?

Although the USCIS conducts periodic webinars, there is not, in fact, any special training required to be able to complete this verification task. It is advisable to be familiar with the form and the tasks required of you as an employer's authorized representative.

How can I get started?

Include this service on your webpage and all social media. Consider contacting local businesses directly to make them aware that you offer this service.

Wedding Officiant

What is it?

A wedding officiant performs a marriage ceremony and is responsible for gathering the appropriate information and signatures to file with the vital records division of the jurisdiction in a timely manner.

What qualifications are needed?

Although there are no special requirements to become a wedding officiant, a notary may apply through the state for permission to perform a marriage ceremony. Florida, Maine, Nevada and South Carolina authorize commissioned Notaries to perform marriage ceremonies as part of their official duties. In Nevada, a commissioned Notary may conduct a maximum of five marriage ceremonies per year once approved.

Because procedures and requirements vary by state, be sure to check with your state administrator for specific policies regarding becoming ordained through an online ministry, as well as for performing religious versus civil and non-denominational ceremonies.

How much does it pay?

Fees vary by state and some states do not specify at all the amount to be charged for officiating a wedding. In some states, the fee charged may be dependent on the state law, and the date and time of the ceremony. For example, in Florida, a notary may charge $20 while in Nevada the fee is $75 to conduct a marriage ceremony. In South Carolina, a notary may charge a $5 notarial fee and a separate travel fee.

How can I get started?

> Depending upon your state, the county clerk or the notary-regulating agency will be able to guide you in determining the specific rules surrounding officiating weddings. Consider consulting your church or other religious affiliation to determine your eligibility as well.

Immigration Forms Specialist

An Immigration Forms Specialist (IFS) is a notary who assists those attempting to enter and live in the United States with the required immigration documentation.

There are many USCIS forms immigrants need help with, like the I-485 (to become a permanent resident or "green card holder") and the N-400 (application for U.S. citizenship). To complete and submit these official forms requires strong English-language fluency and attention to detail.

Technology and the Future of the Notary Public

As we can see, our notary roots have gone through several iterations. From the ancient scribes of Egypt using pigments, water pots and writing implements, to using a wax seal signed with a feather quill. As technology has evolved, the wax seal was replaced by a rubber stamp, and the quill was replaced first by the fountain pen, followed by the ball-point pen.

Now, incorporating technology into the notarial act hopefully ensures that a notary can properly authenticate a transaction. Modern tools that validate identity online, such as credential analysis and knowledge-based authentication, are mature and readily available. Applying a secure e-signature with thorough audit trails of the entire process is now commonplace.

That brings us to **Remote Online Notarization** which allows documents to be notarized in electronic form with the signer using an electronic signature and appearing before a commissioned electronic notary online via audio-video technology. This allows anyone with an Internet connection to get documents signed and notarized online.

What is Remote Notarization?

Remote Notarization is the process by which a notary public conducts a notarial act using audio-visual technology rather than in person. The signer and notary communicate online via webcam, a process otherwise known as online notarization.

Is Remote Notarization the Same as Electronic Notarization?

Many people confuse electronic notarization with remote notarization, believing they are the same. They are not.

Rather than a wet ink signature, electronic notarization, or eNotarization, permits an electronic form to be used for the document signing. In this case, the signer is still required to be physically present with the notary public.

Resources

This page contains trusted connections and resources that you can reach out to. For a complete list and current updates, visit my website at www.sedonanotary.com/becomeanotarypublic.

National Notary Association

http://www.nationalnotary.org

According to reliable industry sources, this is one of America's top choices for **notary** classes, insurance, bonds, stamps and more! Live Customer Support. Satisfaction Guaranteed. Step-by-Step Guidance. Industry-Leading Training. I love this website.

TIP: I highly, highly recommend joining the National Notary Association (NNA). There is a myriad of benefits, including, but not limited to:

- NNA Hotline: Get answers to all your notarization questions from industry experts.
- Education and Training
- Subscription to the National Notary Magazine
- Real-Time Compliance Guide
- Timely New Law Alerts
- Industry Resources
- Discounts
- Downloadable Notary Certificate Forms
- Partner Program Discounts

Secretary of State

Your Secretary of State may have training and/or online seminars.

Notary Public Associations

National Notary Association - www.nationalnotary.org

American Society of Notaries - https://www.asnnotary.org/

Notary Coaching

Bill Soroka Sign and Thrive Notary Training Course and Community

- Notary Signing Agent and Reverse Mortgage Courses, coaching and mentoring https://www.notarycoach.com/course.
- Bill is a breath of fresh air in the profession. He is honest, transparent, available and so likeable. He has been a Notary Public for years, has a very special charism, one that elicits immediate trust. He sincerely cares for his students. The education and training he provides is of the highest quality and industry recognized. His monthly subscriptions rates are nominal, as well.

Notary2pro - Professional Signing Agent Training

- Carol Ray is the founder of Notary2pro. She and Bill Soroka will often team up to provide weekly, live online training and questions/answers. She and her team offer basic and advanced Notary Signing Agent and Reverse Mortgage Courses, coaching and mentoring. Upon graduation, her graduates are recognized as having the knowledge, skills and confidence to complete error free signings. https://www.notary2pro.com/

Facebook Groups

Sign and Thrive Notary Training and Networking Group

Sign & Thrive Notary Training & Networking Group (Members Only)This group is specifically designed to collaborate on ideas, training, business and personal development. Bill fosters an incredible online community of caring notaries, where information, tips and resources are mutually exchanged. You must be a Sign and Thrive member of Bill Soroka's coaching membership.

Notary Reviews, The Good, Bad and the Ugly

https://www.facebook.com/groups/notaryreviews/about/ FB group for notaries public who currently work as Notary Signing Agents.

Software, Tips and Additional Resources

Please visit <u>www.sedonanotary.com/becomeanotarypublic</u> **for up-to-date, industry relevant information on the following subjects:**

- Accounting, printing and CRM Software
- Mobile scanner apps
- Digital thank you cards
- Social Media Pages
- Coaching Programs
- Recommended equipment, including printers and scanners
- National Notary Association Newsletters and articles
- Resource links
- Mileage tracker apps

Office Supplies and Equipment Recommendations

As a *mobile* notary, you'll generally need 6 basic items:

- Pen (blue/black)
- Certificates (Acknowledgements, Jurats, Copy Certifications, etc.)
- Your official seal
- Journal for keeping a record of your notarizations. Although most states do not require a Notary to maintain a journal, it is recommended for the protection and security it affords for both the Notary and the public.
- Printer
- Briefcase

Loan Signing Agent

In addition to the equipment and supplies mentioned above you will need the following:

- Obviously, a smartphone (Android/iPhone)
- Computer and/or laptop
- Dual-tray laser printer and toner (you will be able to print both letter and legal documents)
- Scanner
- Internet connection

Office Supplies

- Legal/letter sized paper
- Blue and black pens
- Paper clips
- Large document clips

On this page I have attempted to lay out general, business and equipment recommendations and tips. This list is not inclusive by any means. For an updated, ever evolving list, please refer to www.sedonanotary.com/becomeanotarypublic.

Summary

So now you have learned about me, the history of the notary practice, the practicality of the business, the process of getting started, how to further your training and education, marketing ideas, plus invaluable resources for you to get up and running quickly and inexpensively as a notary public. Below is a blueprint of the process:

The Nutshell!

1. Get your Notary commission
2. Join the NNA. This will get you access to notary experts that are just a phone call away.
3. Join Bill Soroka's Sign and Thrive community: www.notarycoach.com or www.notary2pro.com. These 2 companies truly set the bar on the highest level of professionalism, honesty and giving back.
4. Get your business cards
5. Publish a keyword enabled website
6. Purchase your office supplies and equipment
7. Implement a CRM application (Customer Relations Management)
8. Start handing out, placing business cards (see list above) and forming relationships with other notaries, escrow and mortgage companies.
9. If you decide to pursue a Loan Signing Agent career, the notary coaches I mentioned above can help and their fees are nominal.
10. Set a routine or a schedule that you follow every day
11. Visit and Bookmark www.sedonanotary.com/notarypublic for current industry related information equipment, resources, etc.

Like most things in life, you have to work at it. With that said, this is a viable business that you can step into with very little money and you can do it part time. Go for it!

Thank YOU and may God bless you.

Epilogue

My heartfelt prayer is that **you** find the information contained in this book inspiring, revelatory and practical. It is sincerely provided in hopes that it can help you have or find a life filled with hope, joy, freedom and financial security.

This manuscript wellsprings from the word "Commissioned" which I have used throughout as a double entendre; unifying to the reader, my life as a humble commissioned follower of Christ and as a commissioned notary public. Believe.